# In Touch With Spirit

## The Shamanic Journey: Workbook 1

### Lower World & Upper World Journey
### Power Animals & Helping Spirits

**Gwilda Wiyaka, CSI**

Berthoud, CO
www.FindYourPathHome.com
303-775-3431

© 2004, 2011, 2012 Gwilda Wiyaka
Path Home Media & Publishing
Berthoud, CO

www.FindYourPathHome.com
TouchIn@FindYourPathHome.com
303-775-3431

All rights reserved. This book may not be reproduced in whole or in part, without written permission from the publisher, except by a reviewer who may quote brief passages in a review; nor may any part of this book be reproduced, stored in a retrieval system, or transmitted in any form or by any means: electronic, mechanical, photocopying, recording, or other, without written permission from the publisher.

| | |
|---|---|
| Cover design: | Gwilda Wiyaka<br>Trixie Phelps |
| Cover photograph: | Shutterstock® Images |
| Illustrations: | Gwilda Wiyaka |
| Prepared for publication: | Trixie Phelps |
| Photographs: | Laura Curtsinger<br>Heather Miller |

## Dedication

To my children, Laura & Jason Curtsinger and Mark and Heather Miller, for their unwavering love faith and support.

To all of my clients, students, and spiritual teachers without whom this workbook could not have been written.

# Table of Contents

Forward ............................................................................................................................. iii

Chapter I: Shamanism ........................................................................................................ 1

Chapter II: The Journey State of Consciousness ............................................................... 3

Chapter III: Introduction to Power Animals and Helping Spirits ...................................... 9

Chapter V: Preparing Your Space .................................................................................... 15

Chapter VI: How to Journey ............................................................................................ 17

Chapter VII: Navigating in Non-Ordinary Reality .......................................................... 21

Chapter VIII: Divination Journeys ................................................................................... 27

Chapter IX: Journey Assignments ................................................................................... 33

Chapter X: Power Animals and Helping Spirits .............................................................. 37

Chapter XI: Power Animal and Helping Spirit Assignments .......................................... 41

About Path Home Shamanic Arts School ........................................................................ 45

About Path Home's State Certification ............................................................................ 47

Resources ......................................................................................................................... 49

CDs and MP3s available for this workbook .................................................................... 49

Additional books, CDs, and MP3s by Gwilda .................................................................. 49

# Forward

The material presented here has not been drawn from any one tradition. Shamanic practices have been discovered in most if not all indigenous cultures around the planet. The Sioux designed their ceremonies and healing practices on certain universal principles, as did the Choctaw, as did the Celts, as did the Druids, as did the Mayans.

It all leads back to the original or universal "way". It is through drawing on these principles that all spiritual healing practices and ceremonies were originally built, be they Aboriginal, Siberian, or Tibetan. In this work, you will draw upon the basic principles also found in other traditions such as power animals, the elements, and the powers of the four directions.

While we use principles that are common to various traditions, we are mindful not to appropriate the ceremonies themselves. These ceremonies were built by the medicine men and women of a particular tribe or nation for their people at that time. Many of the native peoples on our planet, who have preserved and practice the ancient methods, understandably object to societies who first tried to destroy their ways and now borrow freely from their sacred ceremonies.

While we honor where the traditions have come from, and are thankful that our brothers and sisters had the foresight to preserve the old ways, ultimately we honor where it is all going, which is back to center and to that which we all share. It's time for us to come back together, the future of the Earth and all who live upon her depends upon it.

It is not my intent to appropriate the sacred ceremonies of our indigenous brothers and sisters but rather to use the principles offered by life itself to help the student build their own ceremonies. You will learn to design your practice using tried and true universal principles in order to construct what is needed for your personal practice today, tomorrow, and in the future.

# Chapter I:
# Shamanism

Shamanism is an ancient healing practice that is at least 30,000 years old and may date back as far as 50,000 years. It has been practiced in Siberia, Asia, Europe, Australia, Africa, Indonesia, North and South America, and contains elements that are remarkably similar across cultures.

One of the intrinsic elements common to all shamanic practices is a measurable altered state of consciousness known as the journey trance. This trance is much like an interactive dream and is achieved through various ritualistic ceremonies usually employing some form of boring repetitive sound or motion. It was for this purpose that, among many other instruments, ceremonial drums, rattles and didgeridoos were built. Dancing, chanting, or gazing into one of the four elements such as a fire, crystal, or water is sometimes involved.

Such a state of consciousness would be labeled fantasy in our culture. However, to the ancient shamans, it was all a matter of perspective because when in the journey state, the material world appeared to be fantasy. What set the shaman apart from the rest of the tribe was that he or she could easily move between these two states of consciousness at will.

Using this altered state of consciousness, shamans could connect with spirit guides in the metaphorical form of animals, trees, ancestors, and a variety of other spiritual sources such as archetypical gods and goddesses. They could then gain information or guidance for the tribe or any of its members. These spiritual sources could also aid the shaman in performing physical, emotional, mental, or spiritual healing.

The shaman became the conduit through which spirits could enter our ordinary reality to effect healing. Spirits were purported to always be there and willing to help but had to be asked before they could intervene.

In the following chapters, we will be providing information and exercises to help you begin to formulate your own ways of bringing spirit back into your life and your practice.

# Chapter II:
# The Journey State of Consciousness

An indispensable tool for any shaman is the ability to travel into other realms and realities to meet with spirit guides, power animals, ancestors, and spiritual teachers to receive guidance, information, and to perform spiritual healings. Only a few tribes have used hallucinogenic substances to achieve a state of consciousness that would facilitate taking such a journey. The majority of the ancients used some form of rhythmic sound the beating of a drum, the shake of a rattle, or a repetitive chant to name a few.

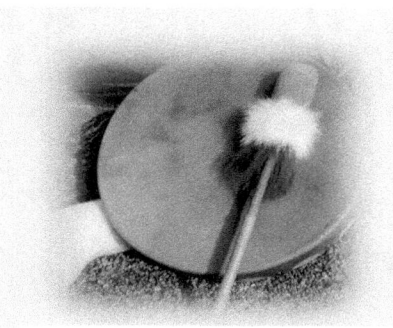

**A Drumbeat Away**

Eyes close, drums sound
Animals come
My spirit leaves my body

Not awake nor sleeping
Visions, dreams

That rewrites the past
That tells the future

Untold freedom
Natural laws bend
Time is not

I am all
And yet nothing

What mystery is this?
Just a drumbeat away
Across the veil

Across the galaxy
Yet contained
Inside my being

~ Gwilda Wiyaka ~

## What Is Journeying?

When we go into a journey state, research has shown that our brain wave frequency drops down to closely match that of the earth at 7.5 Hz. Journey is literally a measurable altered state. A drumbeat or other rhythmic sound or motion is used to help alter our consciousness. The drumbeat also represents our heartbeat, and helps us align with ourselves via the original sound from the womb.

There is a definite parallel between journeying and meditating. Research on Zen monks has shown that those most proficient at meditation were able to slow down their brain waves to within the theta range (4-7 Hz).

Ordinary and Non-ordinary realities were coined by the author Carlos Castaneda and serve our purposes well in describing altered states of consciousness:

**Ordinary reality** - the world we usually live in and which all agree is real.

**Non-ordinary reality** - where the shaman travels on journeys and where rules of time and space that govern our (ordinary reality) world don't apply.

All of us actually already know how to journey. We experience spontaneous journeys all the time. For instance, have you ever have thought of a friend just before receiving a phone call from that same person? That person is thinking of you or they wouldn't be calling you. When they set their intent to go to the phone and call you, they literally journeyed to you with their intent. They popped into your mind because you may have been somewhat in the journey state yourself and sensed their intent as it entered your personal field.

In ancient times when shamanism was more common and journeying more controlled and intentional, people likely had a lot more communication at the non-verbal level and across distances.

Daydreams you've had that later come to pass are also a form of journeying. When we drop into our imagination, we are more likely to receive spiritual information that is not bound by time or place as the imagination is the channel through which spiritual information comes to us. Our sleeping dreams are yet another form of journey. In formal journeywork what we do is choose when we will journey, and then go and return consciously.

We all journey more than we know. It is actually a natural state for us, but we have ceased to recognize what it is and when we do it. Some of us tend to be in journey space more and here less and are often seen as "spacey" or "out there". These individuals also tend to have uncanny intuition at times. Others tend to be here in ordinary reality more and "out there" less having a firm grip on "linear reality" and tend to be well grounded. So some of us will use journey skills to get into journey space, while others use it to gather ourselves and ground back into ordinary reality what we have accessed in non-ordinary reality. There is no right way, but the challenge for those of us who want to be able to access the sacred and bring it into our world is to be able to reliably walk both worlds at will.

A journey is like an interactive or lucid dream during which you are awake and can direct the dream or journey to some extent. However, it is not like a guided visualization in which you can pre-plan and predict what will happen at each stage. In a journey you can choose your actions unlike in a dream but as for the landscape and what you will encounter, you are essentially along for the ride.

During journeys, information comes through our imagination channels. In our culture we tend to socialize children to discount their imaginations by telling them it is not real. Yet our imagination is the channel through which our creativity comes. You cannot manifest that which you cannot imagine.

Imagination is actually a two way street. We first dream or imagine that which we wish to create or manifest and then move it from the void into the world through our will. The other way imagination works is as a receptor and translator of information from non-ordinary reality through our dreams (waking or sleeping) and through the shamanic journey.

The imaginary playmates and invisible animals that many of us played with as children, often relegated to the land of make believe by parents and other adults, are often who we will contact during journeywork. They really were there as our spirit helpers and power animals, and they have likely been with us since we were born.

Sometimes we are more conscious of having these spirits around us than at others, but we witness the results of their presence all the time. How can we explain why more people don't die on our highways every day? Statistically speaking, the odds are definitely against us.

I remember when I first started to journey. I fully expected it to be like Hollywood, complete with full Technicolor, special effects and sound track. I invalidated my journeys for quite a while because they were such a familiar format. It was much like daydreaming.

As it turns out, spirit comes to us through what we have available. Our own personal wiring if you will.

If you are normally a visual person, the journey will tend to come through predominantly in the visual medium. Likewise, if you are mostly auditory the information may, for the most part, be "heard," and if you are kinesthetic it might feel like a knowing or feeling or empathizing with what is going on.

Most of us receive the information through a combination of these channels, but one will be more predominant. As you gain more experience doing journeywork, you may be able to intentionally move the information through particular channels. Also, when you are doing spiritual work for someone else, you may find yourself experiencing in a mode that more suits the other person's wiring as you are, in effect, in their space rather than your own.

We all have the capacity to experience in any one of the modes, and the more you do journey work, the more you can refine them all. In the beginning of your practice, expect the information to mostly come into the channel that you already operate on. Things flow along the path of least resistance.

**Rules of the Road**

At this point in our discussion of journey work we need to address integrity. The good news about journey work is that it really works. The challenge is that it really works.

Any time we contemplate engaging in a practice that has a profound effect on our world we need to formulate responsible guidelines under which to operate in order to not violate the rights of others. As this practice deepens, so do the checks and balances but for now the following are the basic guidelines that will keep you in integrity and out of trouble.

1) We never journey on behalf of another person without obtaining explicit permission.

2) We never journey in order to gain information about another without obtaining explicit permission.

3) The information obtained for another through journey work is sacred and not to be shared with anyone other than the individual you journeyed for without obtaining explicit permission.

4) While we may offer guidelines for dealing with metaphor to those unfamiliar with the process, journeys are to be interpreted only by the individual for whom we journeyed.

5) Journey information is to be used to help ourselves or those we journey for make more informed decisions-- not to make those decisions for us. How we live our lives remains entirely up to us and we are responsible for our actions.

**Is This Real?**

One of the most harmful things we, as a culture, do to our children is tell them that something from their experience is only their imagination and not real. As we just mentioned, it is actually through the channels of our imagination that all spiritual information comes to us. It is also through our imagination that we move out into the world all the things that we care to manifest. To discount our imaginations is to stifle our creativity, block spiritual information that is our birthright and cripple our ability to manifest that which we need or desire in our lives.

When you are on a journey, it may be hard to believe that you are not just making the information up. It can be confusing because you are and you aren't. Any time you engage your imagination; you are either receiving information or creating it. The received information can feel very much like something you have personally dreamed up. What is actually happening is your imagination is receiving spiritual information then creating a metaphor in order to translate the unified spiritual information into a polarized, ordinarily reality format.

Even if it feels like you are making it up, keep journeying and simply note and remember your experiences. Often you will be validated later when you receive information you had no way of knowing and your client or later personal experience verifies it. These experiences will happen more frequently than you might imagine, and, over time, will help you gain confidence in your practice.

Interestingly, an entire group of people can journey to spirit on the same question, and when they bring all their information together it can come together almost like a picture puzzle, containing beautiful and useful truths for all. In these situations, the "true" answer does not belong to any one person, but blends together to form a larger answer.

The question arises, who is this "spirit" we are consulting? (Now bear in mind the following is just truth to the degree of my current understanding and personal evolution.) I have come to realize that there is a continuum that runs from the individual, to their subconscious, unconscious higher conscious, higher selves, then to the collective consciousness of mate, family, community, planet and finally to the creator or the spirit that moves through all things. It is my belief that when I am consulting "spirit" on the behalf of another person I am also consulting their higher selves.

# The Metaphorical Nature of the Shamanic Journey

> **Journey Where?**
>
> The only way
> To truly understand
> The journey process
> Is to relinquish our ideas
> Of the way life is
>
> Do I journey
> Into my own subconscious
> Or to another world?
>
> Yes and yes
> For we ultimately
> Are one
> With all that is
>
> Wake up
> To the beauty and totality
> Of that
> And breathe a breath
>
> Of God
>
> ~ Gwilda Wiyaka ~

One of the challenges of the shamanic journey as a source of information is our own polarized mind set and language. Spirit is not polarized. Also, we as individuals have a limited view and understanding of any subject as compared to the overview available to the spirit that moves through all things.

Our ability to bring accurate information and guidance is thus limited by our belief systems, judgments, and level of understanding.

One of spirit's favorite ways of working around this limitation of mortal man and woman is by the use of metaphor to get concepts across the veil between unity and polarization.

This is also the same operating system we encounter in interpreting our dreams.

Once, when I was a fledgling journeyer just starting to get quite full of myself and my ability to access information from the other side, I was journeying for a friend who was considering breaking up with her boyfriend who, as she put it, had begun to "bore her to tears."

With great confidence I journeyed to lower world and asked what it was that my friend needed to know about her relationship. When I got there, suddenly I was riding my horse flogging her with a crop until she literally dropped dead. I was mortified! I had killed my beautiful power animal, my lovely white mare that was laying there starting to look suspiciously like a mule with Xs in her eyes.

I was so upset it took me a good week to get the courage to show my face in journey space again. When I did, there was my horse as right as rain.

"I thought I had killed you" I wailed. She just pranced around me ready for our next adventure.

It took me another week to realize that my friend's answer to her question (what did she need to know about her relationship) was she was flogging a dead mule.

In journey work the information from spirit has to be translated into a form that is understandable by our polarized minds in ordinary reality. This is done by a series of steps. First the spiritual information is presented to us via the imagination into the un-polarized or more circular portion of our minds or our right brain. If we try to figure out the meaning at this point, more often than not, we miss the point. It is most effective if we just set the events to memory, return from the journey and then journal and/or speak the story. This runs it through our "logical" or polarized linear mind, the left brain, into ordinary reality via language. The journey story can then be interpreted into ordinary reality with meaning intact, sealed in the content of the story line and metaphor.

Information you get on a journey can be metaphorical, literal or, most commonly, a combination of the two. By journaling the information as soon as you return and then relating it back to the question at hand, we can glean the information we need. Often times it is the very act of working with the information in this manner that brings enlightenment or an opening of some closed view we may have held.

This is why when journeying for someone else you not do the interpreting for him or her. You can help them learn to work with metaphor but ultimately they must arrive at the interpretation for themselves. Often the process is more valuable than the answer.

In the "dead mule" case presented above the metaphor may have had much more meaning than the woman was wasting her time with the relationship. The message that she was trying to get more out of the horse/mule than it could provide and that it was quite hurtful to both of them, were both contained in the simple image. This metaphor may have helped her receive additional information in a gentle and non-threatening way.

It is important that we never journey on behalf of another without permission or assume we can give them the interpretation of a journey taken on their behalf.

An exception to this is if you are a health care practitioner and you are journeying on how best to treat your patient. If a person comes to you as a professional and asks for help, it is assumed you may use any and all of your skills in order to provide that help. The patient does not need to know where or how you receive your information any more than a doctor needs to reveal every medical text he or she may consult on a case. Also, if we are asking, "How can I best serve this person," the question really relates to us and how to use our skills. This also is a question we may ask as parents or friends for we are not asking about an individual but rather how we can help, if at all.

If, on the other hand, we ask, "Is my son involved with drugs?" we are violating another's space no matter how well meaning our concern.

# Chapter III:
# Introduction to Power Animals and Helping Spirits

Who are the aforementioned helping spirits and power animals that go with us on journeys, and provide us with information and guidance? According to the ancient shamans, there are helping spirits and power animals that surround us at all times. Some of them come with us when we come into the world, and leave when we leave. Others come and go depending on what energies we need to support us in our lives. Although some of us may not actually see them, there can be a clear sense that they are there with us.

Our power animals can inform us and protect us in ordinary reality, they can balance our energy fields, and they provide a particular energy frequency that we operate most proficiently under in the spiritual realm. They are our guides and consultants when we enter journey space.

The spiritual energies of any power animal are aligned with the universal energies of their species, and therefore carry the particular gifts of that species. For instance, a skunk is known to help us with boundaries. No one harasses a skunk because it is likely they will spray you if you do. So if you were working with boundary issues, it wouldn't be a surprise to have skunk show up as a power animal.

Normally, we have more than one animal at a time. All power animals have equal power, skunk is no greater or less than an eagle other than that it would bring a different expression of power to you. It depends what you need in your life at that time.

If you have a strong affinity for certain animals, they may very likely be your power animals, although other animals may also come to you even though you've had no relationship with them before. Also, if you've ever done a kindness for an animal, such as rescuing them or helping them heal from an injury, it is very possible that it or its species will become one of your power animals.

You may actually see different forms of the same species. In other words, if your animal is a horse, you may see different horses at different times. Ultimately, it may be the horse nation that has come to help you, rather than any one individual horse.

The power animals that come with us and stay until we leave this life are more personal animals that speak of what we came to do in the world. Being able to journey and access these energies or power animals that came with us can help us discover our purpose.

# Chapter IV:
# The Landscape of Non-Ordinary Reality

There are three levels to reality encountered during journeys that seem universal across indigenous cultures: lower world, middle world, and upper world. Different cultures call them different things, and some described non-ordinary reality as more seamless but the principles remain the same.

In some cultures, shaman indicate they used percussion to "travel" to these worlds, while in other cultures the drumming or rattling was viewed as bringing these worlds to the shaman. Ultimately, non-ordinary reality is always present. We simply use the practice to enter a state of consciousness through which we can access it. The percussion brings us into an altered state of consciousness whereby we can access what is already there. Spirit is always with us.

Middle world is the reality we live in, but exists outside of time and space. Therefore, it can be used to travel to another location (astral projection), to our past (regression), or to our futures (divination). Both upper and lower world seem to be landscapes of our unconscious mind as individuals, of the collective mind, and also encompassing all that is, depending on where we set our intent to journey. Lower world appears more grounded and earth-based, while upper world gives the impression of being more ethereal.

The upper and lower worlds may not necessarily always look the same each time you go, although you may run across the same basic landmarks consistently. Sometimes it is totally new and different, and you are taken to a place you've not been before because it is the most expedient way for spirit to get the information to you. Also, when you change geographical locations in ordinary reality and do journey work there you may see some new landscapes based upon the differing longitudinal and latitudinal energies present.

Both upper and lower world are beyond the veils bordering middle world, and both are places you can go to obtain accurate and consistent spiritual information and healings. When you know how to journey to both, simply ask your power animal or spirit guide where would be the best place to journey to get what you have requested, and they will direct you to the most efficient place to obtain it.

## Middle world

Middle world is the reality we are all in, but outside of time and space. As mentioned before, when we think about a friend, and they call us shortly after that, that is a middle world journey at work. Our friend journeyed in middle world and entered our space with their intent to call.

Because middle world is not restricted to time and space, you can take a journey in the middle of winter only to end up in a summertime scene. You can also journey to a past event and collect part of a person's essence left there. This is a healing known as middle world soul retrieval. Interestingly, you can go into your future and meet yourself there. For instance, if you have a future event coming up, you can journey to the space where you will be and already start preparing that space to support your project even before you come into it.

We use middle world to journey to and from our entry point into lower or upper world. Middle world journeys can also be used to ask permission to do shamanic work for someone who is unable to give consent, such as an infant or someone in a coma. Ask your power animal to take you to where that person is located in middle world, and then talk to the person's higher self. Let them know who you are and who has requested that you work with them, and then ask for permission.

Sometimes, when you're requesting to do work for someone in a coma, their higher self may tell you that they are just sticking around long enough for the family to get used to the idea that the person is going to leave. In this case, it would be inappropriate to do healing work on their behalf. This is why you ask. However, even if the person is dying, you may be called upon to do some other kind of healing for them that may be beneficial to them in the dying process. The main point is to never work without permission and to only do what is approved by the client as well as your power animals and helping spirits.

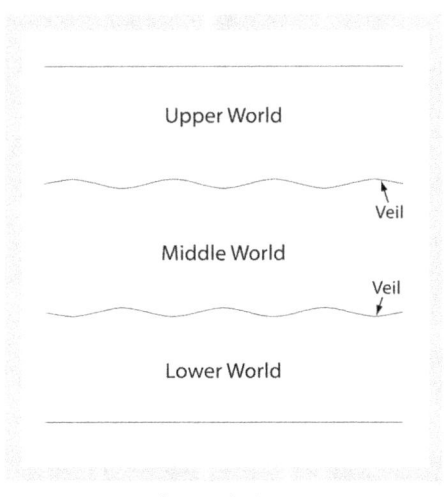

Figure A-1

There is a veil between middle world and upper and lower worlds (see Figure A-1). We cross that veil during a lower world journey when we go down through the earth and during an upper world journey when we go past the sky. Once you've crossed the veil, anyone you meet there you can trust.

Your power animals and spirit helpers are accessed and brought back from the other side of the veil, either from upper world or lower world, and can be trusted even if you access them later in middle world.

However, in middle world there are a lot of disembodied spirits hanging around who may not know they're dead or are afraid to cross over.

People who believe they have not lived a good life and also believe that hell is the result of the life they have lead may be afraid to cross over. Other times people die a sudden death in an accident or while under anesthesia and don't even know they are dead. People in our culture often hold onto the dead because they don't know how to mourn. Because, as a culture, we have moved away from the shamanic practices of our ancestors we find ourselves left with little provision to help the dead cross or for the survivors to consciously release them to do so.

In many Native American traditions mourning was loud and intense, yet brief. Once the mourning was done, the person's name was never spoken again. Instead the deceased was referred to as the brother of my wife or husband of my sister. They believed that to speak the name of the deceased too frequently prevents them from crossing over completely. There is much wisdom in that.

Most all indigenous cultures had some form of a practice used to help souls cross to the other side. In our culture, for the most part, this procedure is no longer practiced. As a result, we may very well have many more misdirected disembodied souls floating around in middle world than in times past.

When people cross over, they cross through the veil, shed all their baggage that isn't who they really are, and become pure spirit. There are some people on the other side, according to all indigenous cultures, who have decided to stay in the between world to help us on our earth walk. Because of this, your spirit guides may sometimes also be your ancestors or someone who was once incarnate.

If you come across a spirit in middle world, remember, as one of my teachers said, "Just because they're dead doesn't mean they're smart." Always have your power animal with you, and if you run across something or someone that wants to talk with you, ask your power animal if this is something or someone that would be in your best interest to listen to or a reliable source of information. Your power animals and helping spirits are all originally retrieved from the other side of the veil, so even in middle world you can trust them. If your power animal indicates it is in your best interest to do so, invite the spirit to meet you in upper or lower world. If they show up there, they are reliable, if not, you can still converse with them, (a practice known as mediumship) but understand they are not any more reliable than any other person in ordinary reality.

Because you need to journey through middle world on your way to upper or lower world, a good rule of thumb is; don't talk to strangers and have a power animal or spirit guide with you that you can ask for guidance and protection. Once you are aware of the identity of one of your power animals, you call the animal to you in ordinary reality and then journey with it. If someone does approach you on your way through middle world, you can turn to your animal and ask if, given your mission and bottom line (which we will discuss later) you need to listen to what is being said or take any action.

Just because there has been a concerted effort to eradicate shamanism in our culture it doesn't mean that the shamanically gifted are no longer being born. There are gifted channels among us that are channeling spirits, but, if these channels are not trained in basic shamanic skills it is not always clear how reliable their sources of information may be. If they are tapping into a spirit in middle world, it could be the alcoholic who died in the gutter down the street who had his own philosophy on things, and still does. He's just not in his body anymore. Because we live in a culture that has no training and apprenticeship for spiritual or shamanic work we may have some very gifted channels who are bringing through very accurate information but of dubious value due to the source they are channeling. If a channel knows to make sure they are either in upper world or lower world, then they can bring in information of much greater value and reliability as well as be clear if they are channeling or serving as a medium.

## Lower World

Lower world is very earth-based and is accessed through the earth by a place where things go underground. For instance, you could access it where water goes underground, or through the roots of a tree, or a cave, a hole, or crack in the ground, an animal den even a tunnel or mine will do in a pinch.

In Celtic tradition, a good access point would be the betwixt and between of nature. That is, any place where one element touches another. For instance, you could use an oceanfront where the earth and the water come together, and journey betwixt and between the two elements into lower world. Or you could use betwixt and between light and dark, sun and shadow, or fire and the wick of a candle.

## Upper World

When we go on an upper world journey first we travel through middle world to get to our launching place, just as we do when we go to lower world. Suitable launching points for upper world tend to be things going up like a tree, mountain, pinnacle, cliff, geyser, or even a fire where the heat rises. The Celts like betwixt and between the horizon and sky at sunrise or sunset.

It is best to choose points that you have a connection with, or have actually been to in the past. For instance, you may use a tree in the yard you grew up in, or one you leaned up against having lunch yesterday. It could be a mountain you have climbed or one you've seen at a distance. It is an actual place in ordinary reality that you have some experience with, which can be used as a jumping off place into upper world.

Upper world often is not as clear and solid or as substantial as lower world.

For this reason I like to have my students practice lower world journeying daily for a week or so before venturing on to the upper world journey.

Journey with your power animal and ask if you are unsure if you have arrived in upper world. As with all things, practice and familiarity will soon dispel doubt.

The landscape tends to be ethereal and sometimes misty or pastel. How you perceive it will greatly depend upon whether you are visual, audio or kinesthetic in nature. Like lower world there is a definite landscape and terrain.

Finding a spirit guide to work with you once you arrive in upper world is rarely difficult. This is because spirit is there waiting for us all the time, and is there to help us as soon as we ask. We live in a free-will universe so spirit cannot impose itself upon us, but they are always anxious to respond when asked.

## Chapter V:
## Preparing Your Space

This is an extensive subject and will be covered at length in Path Home's Sanctuary: Sacred Space: Workbook II (www.FindYourPathHome.com/store.html). For now we will just cover some basic elements to enable you to experience your first journeys in comfort and safety.
It is important that you are comfortable. It is difficult to journey when you are distracted by physical discomfort, say for instance, lying on a hard floor or having a full bladder. Being too comfortable, however, can result in the journey being one into sleep; restful but not overly productive. Choosing a spot where you do not normally sleep, can work well. If you do choose to use your bed, lying sideways rather than in the normal orientation can help your body get it that this is not naptime.

Choose a time and place where you will not be interrupted. Unplug the phone and let family members know you are not to be disturbed for the duration you have chosen for your journey.

Burn sage in the room, light a candle, and set up any sacred objects around you that remind you of your power animals or help you feel at ease.

**Safe Traveling**

Calling in your power.

It is always the first step in any journey work to call in your power animals. The rules of safe travel are:

1. Never travel without your power animals.

2. Don't talk to strangers.

3. Be specific about coming and going (take the same route coming back as you did going).

To call in your power animal you can use some form of percussion, the first portion of the CD or a rattle before you put on your head set. While listening to the drums or rattle ask your power animal to come join you so you can journey. In your imagination, see your power animal enter the room and come to your side.

# Chapter VI:
# How to Journey

You will need:

- Drumming CD or MP3 and (www.FindYourPathHome.com/store.html)
- Personal CD player or iPod with headphones
- Rattle (optional)
- Bandana or eye pillow to cover your eyes
- Throw and pillows for comfort (optional)
- Sacred objects to help set space
- Journal and pen
- A dream symbols book (optional)
- A power animals book (optional)

As mentioned before it is important to find a space in your house where you won't be interrupted. If you are interrupted while on journey you may be left feeling scattered or spaced out. If you've ever been deep into thought, in a daydream, or absorbed in a good book and been interrupted, you may notice that you're spacey for quite a while afterword. What has happened in all of these cases is you are stretched between ordinary reality and imagination or journey space and are not totally present in either.

If you are interrupted, as soon as you get an opportunity, go back to your prepared sacred place and methodically journey back into where you were before you got interrupted. There you can collect yourself, and either go on with the journey or come back out. You may also find yourself feeling scattered if you don't follow the usual methodical way of entering or leaving journey space. You can always ask a power animal to help you if you are feeling scattered. It will let you know if you have left a part of you behind during a journey and then help you go regain it.

When you've lost yourself in journey, it's relatively easy to retrieve yourself. However, when you've lost soul parts through some trauma, you need someone else to go get the pieces for you because the soul parts are usually in a guarded space one cannot enter alone and require personal processing to integrate the soul part back into the whole. This situation requires professional help from a well-trained shamanic practitioner.

Begin the journey process by getting aligned with the spirit world first. In order to get along in the world, we are required to be in ordinary reality a great portion of our lives. So it is important to take steps to make a space where you can start to move into the altered state before you go on a journey. This will enhance the quality and clarity of your journey. For instance, you may surround yourself with sacred objects that represent spirit energy to you. This helps set the intent and the journey.

Unknowingly, we hold off and field all sorts of energies all day long, and this takes up a fair amount of our energy. When you set up sacred space, the sacred space fields the energy so you don't have to. Then you can relax and focus on leaving your body and going on the journey in safety.

At this point you might softly beat a drum or shake a rattle and hum to yourself. All this helps you to gently begin to enter altered state of consciousness.

Once you have set up the space and mood for a journey, use the drumming CD or MP3. Lie down and cover your eyes with a bandanna or other eye covering. Then, call in a power animal or spirit guide to accompany you. If you haven't had a power animal retrieved for you yet, ask for a power animal to accompany you and see who shows up in your "imagination."

A live drummer is wonderful and most certainly can also be used but it is important they are familiar with and well versed in the journey rhythm and call back beat.

State your intention for the journey to your animal or guide. In the following pages you'll be directed to take several journeys during which the intention will be stated for you. Later, you can decide what you want to accomplish during a journey and compose it yourself based on these principles.

Once you've stated your intention, follow your guide to your entry point into lower or upper world. Bear in mind that in journey space you travel in a way that is unlike how you would in ordinary reality, often going as the crow flies and moving very rapidly. It is best to travel a nice direct route that you know you can find later to travel back on. So be as specific as you need to accomplish this. This is very important in more advanced shamanic techniques such as power animal or soul retrieval work so it is best to develop the discipline at the entry level rather than try to relearn later on.

When on journey, a waking dream will unfold for you. Pay attention to all of your senses and learn how spirit best communicates with you. If nothing seems to be happening create it in your imagination. At first this will feel like you are making it up which you are. What you are actually making up is the metaphor through which spirit can communicate with you. Journeying is a cooperative endeavor in which you actively engage your imagination in order to commune with spirit. With time and practice you will see that, though you seemed to be making the journey up, it provided information and guidance you had no way of knowing.

We all have gifts and it is about discovering what your gifts are and how best to use them. As time goes on, you and your power animals and helping spirits will develop your own style. When teaching journey skills, a certified shamanic instructor's main responsibility is to get you to the point that you are getting consistent reliable information from your guides and then your power animals and helping spirits can take over.

When first learning journey skills it may feel awkward and unnatural. With time and practice, it becomes easier and more fluid. To start out with and in the interest of instruction, a generic method is being imposed on your natural ability to journey. This is to set you off in the right direction, as you gain your journey legs, just do as your power animals and helping spirits instruct and you will enjoy the best instruction available and have many wonderful adventures.

It is good to practice journeying as much as you can after you acquire the skills. It is best to start with a fifteen-minute journey. Later you can expand that to thirty minutes. Otherwise, it is hard to keep track of all the information that comes to you. As you become more advanced, sometimes journeys forty-five minutes or even an hour might be useful.

**Initial Journey to Lower World**

15 - minute Journey
(Track 4 on "On Wings of Spirit" or "Betwixt and Between" CDs/MP3s)

Choose a spot in ordinary reality that enters the earth through a place where things go underground. It is best to pick a place you have actually been like a favorite tree in the back yard of your childhood home.

Call in your power animal, introduce yourself, and state that you are there to practice lower world journey and graciously ask for help. You will almost always get an affirmative answer.

Once you perceive that your power animal is with you, imagine yourself sitting up out of your body, and either ride, fly, walk, or even become your animal. Do whatever feels right or your animal shows you to do.

See yourself go with your power animal cross-country to the spot in middle world that you've chosen to be your entry point to lower world. Whether the spot is nearby or far away, it shouldn't take you more than a moment or two to get there.

Once you arrive at your spot, approach it respectfully, introduce yourself and ask for help in making the passage to lower world.

It will show you how. Follow those instructions, while making sure your power animal is with you.

If you are under ground with roots and soil you have not arrived yet. Just keep going until you break out into another landscape.

This is lower world. If you are in doubt that you have arrived, ask your power animal.

Once there, call out for a power animal that is willing to help you, it may be the same animal that accompanied you there or a different one.

Ask for a guided tour of lower world.

If you have any questions or doubts along the way, ask your power animal for guidance.

When the drum sounds the call to return, thank whomever you are talking to and journey back exactly the way you came. This can happen rather rapidly.

If you have not yet fully returned from your journey when the drumming stops continue your methodical retracing of your path until you do.

When you have arrived back at your body, thank your power animal, say goodbye, and see yourself lay down into your body.

Journal everything you remember from your journey as soon as you return.

It is advisable to practice your lower world journey several times before moving on to the upper world journey.

**Initial Journey to Upper World**

15 - minute Journey
(Track 4 on "On Wings of Spirit or "Betwixt and Between" CDs)

Choose a jumping off spot in ordinary reality that you are familiar with. Suitable launching points for upper world are things going up like the branches of a tree, a mountain, a pinnacle, or a geyser,

Call in your power animal, introduce yourself, and state that you are there to practice your upper world journey and that you'd like to meet one of your spirit guides.

Imagine yourself sitting up out of your body and journey in middle world with your animal to your jumping off spot.

Approach it respectfully, introduce yourself and ask for help in making the passage to upper world. Do as it instructs.

You will go up past the sky and the clouds. If you find yourself amidst stars and planets, you are not there yet. Keep going because that is outer space, which is still in middle world.

Beyond outer space you will find a landscape. It might be fairly ethereal. If you are in doubt that you have arrived, ask your power animal.

Call out for a helping spirit that wants to help you with your upper world journeys.

When you see someone arrive, ask if he or she is the one who has come to help you.

Once you've determined that you have found your helping spirit, ask for a tour of upper world.

When the drum sounds the call to return, thank your helping spirit, and journey back with your animal exactly the way you came.

If you have not yet fully returned from your journey when the drumming stops continue your methodical retracing of your path until you do.

When you have arrived back at your body, thank your power animal, and see yourself lay down into your body.

Journal everything that you can remember.

## Chapter VII:
## Navigating in Non-Ordinary Reality

It is possible to start in lower world and end up in upper world. Our souls do indeed go to the edge of the earth and beyond. Power animals and helping spirits can be in both places at once.

Whenever you encounter anything unusual during a journey, you can always ask your power animal or spirit guide for guidance. You don't need to fear that something bad will happen to you because the basic instructions for taking a journey are designed to create a safe space for you to explore non-ordinary reality.

At some time or another, you may experience sexual feelings during a journey. Our culture has many judgments and unhealthy attitudes around sexuality, but spirit has no problem with it. Orgasm is a form of moving energy and sometimes we experience this on a journey. If you can go with the process and let go of your judgments around it, it can bring a very powerful healing. Culturally speaking, the root chakra is where we carry most of our damage. Our sexuality has been so maligned that it vibrates slower than it is designed to and this experience can serve to realign our chakras. That is part of the cause of gynecological and prostrate problems. The energy is stuck and the sexual journey can help release the restrictions often found there. So go with it and have a good time! Just be sure to lock up your journal. (Just kidding.)

Another interesting phenomenon is when we are commandeered while on journey and given a healing even when we didn't directly ask for one. This will not happen if we are not opened to it and the permission isn't there. Know that choices you have made and things you have set in motion with your intention may be fulfilled when you enter non-ordinary reality. When you receive a spiritual healing very often you'll feel it in your body, mind, and emotions or any combination of the three, as well as in the spiritual realm.

Dismemberment journeys, where you are ripped limb from limb and cast off in the four directions, gobbled up by power animals, burnt up in fire, or any other form of dismantling, are usually considered to be initiatory. They can sometimes be very frightening. Those who are fairly gifted and have set an intention that indicates a commitment or dedication to healing work and serving spirit can encounter these journeys. When you have made such a commitment, often spirit will energetically take you apart and then put you back together again in rapid fashion. This work is presented as a dismemberment to metaphorically convey to you what is happening at an energetic level and is not meant to harm or frighten you.

During a journey you may also come across someone from ordinary reality that you know or have known. There are many reasons why this might happen. Often it is someone who has your best interest at heart and is covering, surrounding, or protecting you energetically in some way.

Or it may be someone you are enmeshed with or have had a spirit or energy exchange with. Seeing them in your journey space may be a metaphoric way of relaying that information to you.

When we go into journey space, particularly for the first time, sometimes it is like coming home to some place that you've wanted to be for so long. This may make it hard to leave journey space and come back to ordinary reality and you may experience a sense of homesickness. The beauty is that now you have the skills necessary and can always go back.

**To Where Do We Journey?**

This is a question that if you ask two hundred different shamans you would get two hundred and one different answers, all of which would be true.

Where we are journeying to is and isn't into our own unconscious, and it is and isn't into the collective unconscious, and it is and isn't into all that is. The Celts and Druids believe that our soul extends to the ends of the earth and beyond. This seems to be the case when you journey because sometimes, when you journey for a person, you find that you have journeyed into that person's landscape and can access things that only that person could know about. That is an experience where it seems you have journeyed into another's unconscious. Yet, you may also have gathered that information from the collective unconscious or from the source of all that is.

It is likely that when working on behalf of someone else, you're journeying into his or her unconscious mind. Similarly, if you journey on your own behalf, you go into your own unconscious. Be aware that, in many systems of thought, the flow between your unconscious and that of another's is very seamless, and they both continue on out into the collective or universal unconscious. Ultimately, it seems that there is no real disconnection between the one who created us and ourselves. So this work can be very seamed or segmented, which is good because that is the way we think. But it can also be very seamless and unified.

When you are journeying on behalf of yourself, and ask spirit for answers, you are really talking to your multileveled self. So if your conscious self seeks information, realize that there may be parts of you that don't really want to know. Therefore, our higher selves will feed us the answers that the majority of our selves can accept. If the answer seems incomplete, realize that it may be because you are not fully ready to accept it, and not because spirit won't share it with you. Journeys almost always deepen with meaning as you delve into them. This dynamic nature of the shamanic metaphor is one of the things that make journey work so powerful. You will absorb what you can process at any given time but upon revisiting the journey at a later date, an entire new layer of meaning may open up to you. Keeping your journals and revisiting your journeys is always worth the time and effort.

Journeying is a way in which to reconnect with ourselves and with source so that we have a direct personal line to our own inner sanctuary and own inner knowing. In our culture we stumble and fall and flail around trying to find our way in the world. We go to different places and different people hoping someone will tell us who we are and what we need to do. But ultimately, it is to ourselves, our own connection to all that is, that we must go to find answers and journeying can take us there.

## How to Pose a Question

### The Nature of Reality

Before we can accurately ask and interpret questions it is necessary to reframe the way we view reality.

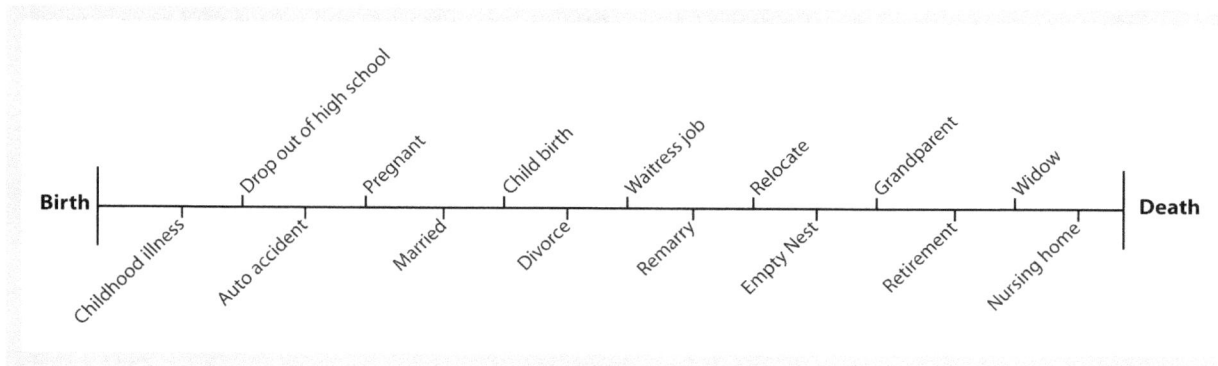

Figure A-2

Because we live in a linear, polarized reality, we tend to think of our lives as linear. We start at birth, follow a predestined path of things that "happen to us," and end at death (see Figure A-2).

This is what our lives have become as a result of our history yet it doesn't have to remain that way.

We actually come with a "set" of paths to choose from. We choose or agree upon this set each time we become incarnated, depending upon what we wish to experience, learn, or accomplish during a particular lifetime. This is where free will enters in (see Figure A-3).

When first embarking upon my spiritual path, I, like many others, was looking for what Spirit wanted me to do. What was I supposed to be? It was quite a shock when I discovered that, "Quite frankly, madam, spirit doesn't give a damn." Every time I asked about my life's path the answer was, "What do you want it to be?" Talk about no guidance or direction! It's a lonely experience to discover we *are* the spirit we serve.

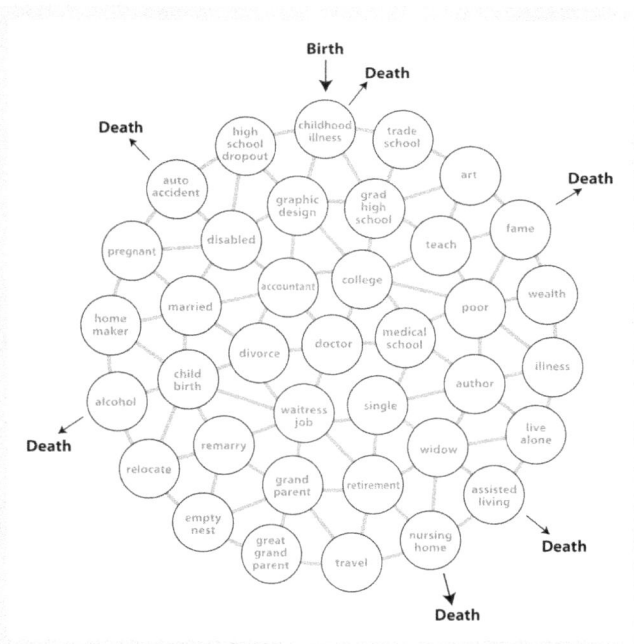

Figure A-3

Eventually I learned that within my given set, my "great purpose" was simply living my life. How I chose to do it was up to me. It sure took the excuse "Spirit made me do it" out of the picture.

This is my life. The choices and results of those choices are up to me. The buck stops here. So where's the glory??? At first I was disappointed that I was not the star of some great plan.

I have since come to realize I *am* the star of some great plan, but I am the planner. There's a lot of freedom and responsibility, in that. On deeper levels, it puts us in the position of being co-creators rather than puppets. Once we get over the shock that we are ultimately responsible for our choices and that the life we are living is entirely the result of our choices, conscious or unconscious, we can truly engage in the process of living.

Let's look at this in a little more detail. As I stated, when we come in, we have a "set" within which we can operate. In this lifetime, I will never be a tall, black, successful basketball player. Wrong race, wrong gender, wrong height, and at this point, wrong age. It is simply not in my set. I suppose I could join a gym and take lessons, but the chance of doing more than spraining an ankle and embarrassing myself is pretty slim. Fortunately (or by design) I have no real passion or desire to be a basketball player.

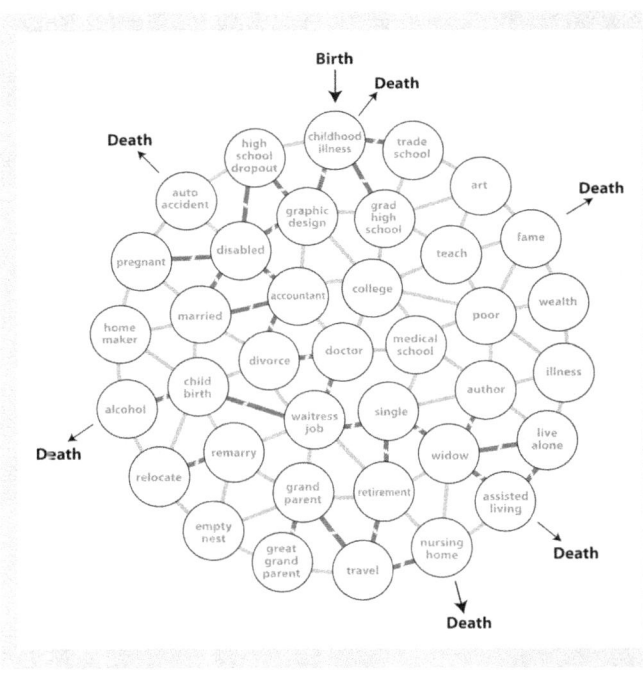

Figure A-4

In the illustration (Figure A-3), consider each circle an "option" and the lines between the circles as "paths" from option to option. This represents the set we come in with. In a perfect world, we would have access to all of our options. As things are, we take a bit of a beating and as a result, we disconnect from some of our options (Figure A-4).

When I incarnated this time, I came as a female. Within that, I had many options. Early on, I was messaged, as many of us are, that being a girl meant I was a second class citizen. If anyone went to college, it would be my brother. If I got to go at all, it would be to find a husband and become a good wife. That's what women did. I would really have loved to be a doctor, and within my set, I could have been a great one.

But I suffered what is called "soul loss" around my ability to pursue a profession that, at the time, was considered to be for men only. This resulted in my disconnecting from many options by taking on that belief. Similarly, we systematically disconnect from our options until what's left is a single path that starts at birth and ends at death, with fairly predictable things happening to us along the way.

My path could easily have been: get married, have children, bring them up, become an empty nester, travel with my husband after he retires, become a widow, and then die. Fortunately, I discovered my set, reconnected with at least some of my original options and am living *my* life, rather than the one I was programmed to live.

I reconnected to many of my options through a shamanic healing modality known as soul retrieval.

**The Bottom Line**

When asking a question of spirit, I always like to come from what I refer to as my bottom line. In other words, what I am and am not willing to experience at this time. This gives spirit a starting point and helps me refine my intention.

An example of a question asked with a bottom line is: "***Given that I want to serve spirit, in health, joy, abundance, ease, and be present for my children when they need me*** what would it look like if I take this new job?"

A bottom line may change from time to time and from question to question, but you will probably find particular elements tend to consistently be included. These are the things that are the most important to you and need to be considered when making decisions and when asking questions to guide these decisions.

It is important to note that if you are fortunate enough to have access to soul retrieval healing you can simply decide what you want and ask: "Given my bottom line and that I wish to obtain_____ (you fill in the blank) what do I need to know, do or heal in order to do so?"

For more information on soul retrieval healing or to find a certified shamanic practitioner see: www.FindYourPathHome.com/practitioners.html

# Chapter VIII:
# Divination Journeys

Journeys may also be used when you are trying to create something professionally or personally. For instance, if you have a report to prepare, or have been commissioned to do some piece of art for someone, or want to give a loved one a gift, you can journey and ask for ideas or what your options are for colors or formats.

If you are contemplating the purchase of a home and want more information upon which to base your decision you can journey and ask what unseen factors you may need to know about.

If you have a health question, you can ask for guidance or advice on how to heal. In fact, you can directly ask for a healing. Know that you must address an illness on all four levels, physical, emotional, mental, and spiritual to effect a healing.

**Journeying on a Question**

Journeys can be used to answer any questions you might have for yourself or with permission, another. The clarity and accuracy of your interpretation of the answer will be greatly affected by how you word the question.

Spirit does not deal well with questions that require a yes or no answer. Nor does spirit deal well with questions that ask whether or not you should do something. Spirit may see the incredible lessons you can learn from, what you would view as, a horrible experience to be grounds enough to answer yes to your question. Needless to say, that may not be what you had in mind.

It is important to use journey work to collect data in order to help you make more informed choices in your life rather than rely on spirit to make your value judgments for you. To excuse your behavior or justify your actions by claiming spirit "told you to do it" is not only manipulative it is disempowering.

Answers will mostly come to you in metaphors, so if you ask more than one question per journey you may not know which metaphor refers to which question. It is best to limit yourself to one question per journey when you are beginning your practice.

Sometimes you may just ask spirit what lessons a certain choice could bring for you and then decide if you want to experience those particular lessons or not.

You always have free will. Spirit doesn't have the same value system or think the same way as we do, nor does it have an investment in how we learn our lessons, so you need to be very specific about how you ask your questions in order not to be inadvertently misled.

Spirit can give you information to base your choices on, yet, there are no right or wrong choices. Ultimately, it is up to us to make the choice and glean the lessons along that particular path. Spirit is not attached to what lessons you have. You will get them one way or another.

If you are trying to help someone in your life, especially someone close to you, when you pose your question to spirit ask what you can do and not what that other person needs to do because that would be journeying into the other person's personal space without permission and is a boundary violation and inappropriate.

Journeying is a way in which to reconnect with ourselves and with source so that we have a direct personal line to our own inner sanctuary and own inner knowing. In our culture we stumble and fall and flail around trying to find our way in the world. We go to different places and different people hoping someone will tell us who we are and what we need to do. But ultimately, it is to ourselves, our own connection to all that is, that we must go to find answers and journeying can take us there.

**How to Pose a Question**

**The Bottom Line**

When asking a question of spirit, I always like to come from what I refer to as my bottom line. In other words, what I am and am not willing to experience at this time. This gives spirit a starting point and helps me refine my intention.

An example of a question asked with a bottom line is: "***Given that I want to serve spirit, in health, joy, abundance, ease, and be present for my children when they need me*** what would it look like if I take this new job?"

A bottom line may change from time to time and from question to question, but you will probably find particular elements tend to consistently be included. These are the things that are the most important to you and need to be considered when making decisions and when asking questions to guide these decisions.

**Taking a Divination Journey**

Call in your power animal, tell it you have a question, and ask to be taken on a journey to be given an answer.

*Ask to be taken to either lower world or upper world depending upon which you are doing this assignment for.*

After you have acquired journey skills to both upper and lower world, allow your power animal to choose the level of reality you will be going to in order to assure you are in the optimum place for receiving the information you are requesting each time.

Once you arrive, everything that happens after that is considered part of the answer. Remember that the answer will most likely come to you in metaphor. It is important not to try to discern the answer to the question while you are on journey. Set the events of the journey to memory, come back and record the journey in your journal before you work on interoperation.

If you are asking the question on behalf of someone else, your role is to record the journey, as you experienced it, and then assist the other person in deciphering the message that makes the most sense to them. Do not interpret the journey for them.

If a meaning seems obvious to you but the other person cannot see it, you are either mistaken or the person is not in a position to gain that information at the time. Ultimately, the best interpretation is the one made by the person asking the question. Often the very act of puzzling through the information on their own leads them to a deeper understanding or even a healing.

**The Art of Journaling**

The shamanic metaphor is sacred spiritual information and like many channeled spiritual works such as the Tao Te Ching, can take on deeper meaning with every reading. Journey information, like the journey itself, is transtemporal in nature and can serve as guidance in and for the future.

Sometimes on journeys we are also given symbols that warrant drawing out in our journals as well. The journaling of your shamanic journeys can be an entire art form in itself. Following are some things I have found most useful over the years of my practice.

I like to start out with a journal book that I find esthetically pleasing and easy to write in. I also have on hand colored pens. Before going on my journey I write down the date, my bottom line and question or reason for the journey in my journal. When I return from the journey I transcribe it writing on every other line in my journal (see Figure A-5).

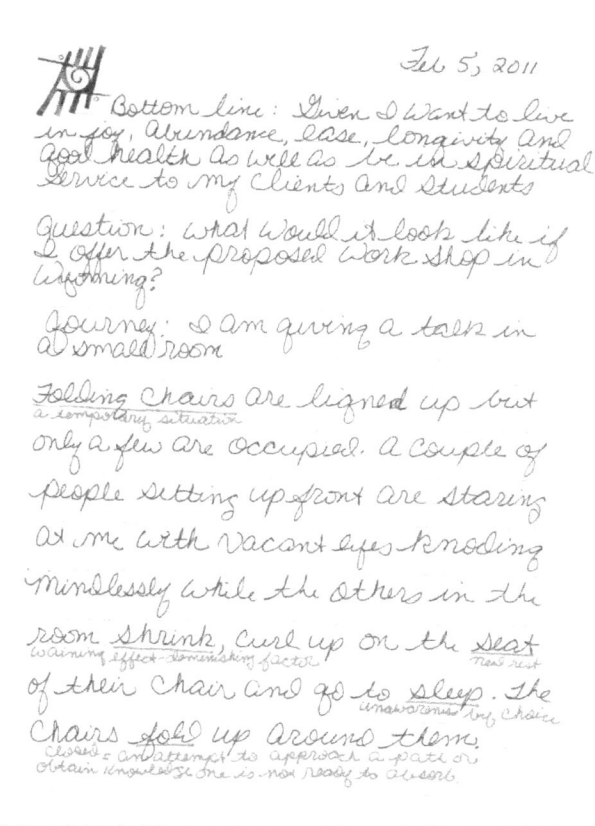

Figure A-5

After writing the journey I will go through it and with one of my colored pens, underlining the words I want to examine metaphorically. It can be useful to have several books to aid you in decoding your journey: A book on power animals and one on dream symbols. Please bear in mind, however, that you, not the books, are the ultimate authority on the meaning of your metaphors. Interpret the journey by translating metaphors and then referring the journey back to your questions and bottom line.

Once I look up the words in a dream journal, or come up with possible meanings, I jot them down in the extra space between the lines in color.

I study the information and possible meanings of the words and symbols and refer it back to my bottom line and question. Once I think I have a fairly accurate understanding of the material, I journal my interpretation below the original journey.

I keep my journals and go over them at special times such as the New Year or my birthdays when I find it useful contemplate my process and give gratitude for my many lessons and blessings.

**Interpreting Journeys**

The information you receive on journey will flow with how you are designed. Some people are very visual, while others are more auditory or kinesthetic. One person may see a vivid scene providing the answers they need, while another will actually hear words, which may sound like their own internal dialogue. If you are kinesthetic, you will probably have more of a felt sense of things.

Some of the information is metaphorical, while some is literal. Spirit may use certain symbols or metaphors it knows to have meaning for you. Again, you can use a book of symbols to guide you in your interpretation, but also realize that the final meaning is what it means to you.

Remember that what you access on journey is probably contents of your own unconscious mind. Hence the choice of metaphors is very personal.

Everything that we experience on journey, including how we respond and feel, what goes through our minds and our physical sensations, is all part of the information.

For instance, you may be journeying for someone and suddenly feel terrified, although there is nothing in the journey that would warrant the fear. This fear may be information for your client that is coming through you emotionally.

If you journey for another person, pay attention to emotions that come up that don't seem to be yours and even the ones that do. It is all valuable information.

There is a biblical passage which suggests that in order to enter the gates of heaven we need to become as little children. Similarly, when we enter into spirit in journeywork, a childlike wonder and innocence is much to our benefit rather than the more ingrained habit of superimposing the events of our past onto an experience, thereby coloring the information.

If the journey doesn't turn out the way you planned or expected, stay with it and become curious. Undoubtedly, you will be pleasantly surprised.

Sometimes journeys pose more questions than they answer. You can start a journal of your journeys and the questions that they pose, and then plan follow-up journeys to find answers.

Dreams can also be a powerful source of information. When engaging in a shamanic practice it is wise to record your dreams as answers posed in journeys may also come to you in your dreams. You may also have the answers come to you during the day in outward signs (omens) or internal intuitions.

Spirit is, by its very nature, unified. It doesn't convert well into the polarized world we have created for ourselves. To spirit, there is no light/dark, good/bad, or right/wrong. When we communicate with spirit, there is a lot of room for us to misinterpret based on our limited polarized view.

Spirit uses the language of metaphor to help translate things into our polarized world. It is kind of like trying to get a PC to talk to a Mac. The language doesn't translate well.

Spirit is trying the best it can to get a common language by using metaphor. It may choose archetypal representations that communicate well to you. This can include storybook characters, people from your past, or universal symbols. For instance, you may see Darth Vader in a journey. Spirit uses things it finds in your unconscious mind that would best represent the concept it is trying to convey to you.

Often, your journey may look meager or not very colorful. Even getting nothing but darkness is an answer.

In the process of translating the metaphors in your journey, it becomes a living thing. This is why it is very important not to judge your journey while it is unfolding in unified reality.

After returning from the journey, carefully write down everything you can remember, and then work with the images.

One of the pitfalls of going on a journey is being tempted to translate it as it is happening and missing some of the meanings. When you're in non-ordinary reality you are no longer the PC anymore. You are the Mac. So you have to come back into ordinary reality with the information as it unfolded, download it into the PC, and then unzip the file, so to speak, in order to make sense of it.

Sometimes your answers will seem very clear to you during the journey. But if you are baffled by the metaphors being used during the journey, you can ask spirit to show you the answer in another way. Do that as much as you need. Spirit is very accommodating.

After you've returned from the journey, you can work with the metaphors to decipher the meaning. This is a lot like working with your dreams so you may use books that interpret dream symbols to assist you.

You can spend literally days with a single journey finding meanings imbedded in it at increasingly deeper levels. You can also journey on your journeys or symbols used in your journey, or your nighttime dreams, to ask for further clarification.

If you journal all of your journeys and then go back in a year and reread them, the meaning will have deepened considerably. This is because you have begun to develop fluency with your communication with spirit. You may also be pleasantly surprised to see how precognitive your journeys have been.

When you journey for another person, be very specific about the details of the journey because there may be metaphors and other information that would make no sense to you but would be very rich information for the other person.

The more you work in the spirit realm, the easier it becomes to apply the principles of spirit's non-polarized reality in our world. For instance, it may become easier to see that some of the people who have hurt you most in your life have also been some of your greatest gifts. For every action there is an equal and opposite reaction.

**What Is Journeying For?**

There are many uses for journey skills. One is to use it to clarify the meaning of a dream. Dream language, like that of journeys, is metaphor. Dreams are valuable gems that can help guide us, just as journeys can.

Sometimes we have dreams that are obviously very important. They may seem more like a vision than a dream and can sometimes have information for us as well as for our community and the people around us. When you sense your dream may carry important information, or if you would just like to further study the meaning of any dream, using journey skills is a powerful way to get more depth in the interpretation.

# Chapter IX:
# Journey Assignments

**Lower World Journey Assignment #1:**

**Journey to Clarify a Dream**

15 - minute Journey (www.FindYourPathHome.com/store.html)
(Track 4 on "On Wings of Spirit" or "Betwixt and Between" CDs or MP3s)

Write down the dream in your journal. Use your books to interpret the dream and write that down as well.

Choose an entry spot in ordinary reality that meets the criteria and that you are familiar with.

Call in your power animal. Let it know that you'd like to obtain an interpretation of your dream, and if needed, specify what aspect of the dream you want clarification on.

Travel to lower world with your power animal according to the instructions you received in Lower World Journey Class.

When you arrive, call out that you are here on your own behalf, or that of another, to obtain an interpretation of your dream about (give a brief description; i.e., the cat on the roof).

Everything that happens after that will be in reference to the dream.

Don't try to interpret the information spirit is giving you while it is unfolding. Just note everything that you experience and journal it when you return.

When you hear the call back beat, journey back the exact way you went and journal the journey as soon as you are back.

You may use the dream symbols and power animal's books to interpret the journey by translating metaphors and then referring the journey back to the dream. Cross-reference the two. This is akin to looking at the dream with two eyes verses one. You get a better view or greater depth perception.

If you are still unsure about the meaning of the dream, you can repeat the exercise and/or ask someone else to go on a journey for you, and obtain additional information for you.

Do this assignment twice; once for yourself and once for someone else.

**Lower World Journey Assignment # 2:**

**Journey on a Personal Question**

15 - minute Journey (www.FindYourPathHome.com/store.html)
(Track 4 on "On Wings of Spirit" or "Betwixt and Between" CDs or MP3s)

Work with wording the question as you were instructed to do in Journey Class. Remember, an answer can only be as good as the question. Also decide on your bottom line as it applies to the question you are asking.

Write both your bottom line and question down in your journal.

Call in your power animal. Let it know that you'd like to obtain an answer to a question you have.

Journey to lower world as you have been taught. When you get there, call out your bottom line and question.

From the point you pose your question, everything that happens will apply to the answer so remember everything you can.

When you hear the call back beat, journey back the exact way you went, and journal the journey as soon as you are back.

Use your books and interpret the journey by translating metaphors and then referring the journey back to your original question and bottom line.


**Upper World Journey Assignment # 1:**

**Journey on an Illness**

15 - minute Journey (www.FindYourPathHome.com/store.html)
(Track 4 on "On Wings of Spirit" or "Betwixt and Between" CDs or mp3s)

Work with wording the question as you were instructed to do in Journey Class. Remember, an answer can only be as good as the question. Also decide on your bottom line as it applies to the question you are asking.

Write them both down in your journal.

Call in your power animal. Let it know that you'd like to obtain an answer to a question you have.

Journey to upper world as you have been taught. When you get there, call out your bottom line and question.

To journey on an illness, take four separate journeys and ask what is the manifestation or cause of the illness in question at each of the four levels.

1. Physical
2. Emotional
3. Mental
4. Spiritual

Then take four more separate journeys and at each level ask how you can best address the illness and support your healing.

From the point you pose your question, everything that happens will apply to the answer so remember everything you can. Remember, only ask one question per journey.

When you hear the call back beat, journey back the exact way you went, and journal the journey as soon as you are back.

Take other journeys and ask specific questions, such as which diet or lifestyle adjustment is best for your condition. It is most effective if you ask such questions again periodically because the answer can change from season to season or year to year.

Use the dream symbols and power animal's books as reference texts to interpret the journey by translating metaphors and then referring the journey back to your original question and bottom line.

*For the above journey assignment you may practice the "in and out journey."*

**The In and Out Journey**

1 - hour Journey (www.FindYourPathHome.com/store.html)
(Track 1 on "On Wings of Spirit" or "Betwixt and Between" CDs or MP3s)

In this journey you are able to ask multiple questions without mixing up the metaphors.

Have your pen and journal close at hand with all the questions you wish to address written one to a page with your bottom lines. Leave plenty of room to journal the journey.

Journey as you normally would to get a question answered. When you have gotten the first question answered, tell whichever power animals or helping spirits you are working with to please wait as you have more questions and will be right back. Journey back with your power animal, quickly journal the journey, read the next question and bottom line and journey back with it. Ask the question and repeat the process.

When you are done, or tired, whichever comes first, you do not have to wait for the call back beat. On your last journey home, be sure to be very specific and methodical. Do something grounding when you return as these journeys can make you spacey until you get used to them and learn your limits. Four questions in a row are usually more than plenty, depending on how complex the journey.

**Upper World Journey Assignment # 2:**

**Healing Journey**

30 - minute Journey (www.FindYourPathHome.com/store.html)
(Track 3 on "On Wings of Spirit" or "Betwixt and Between" CDs or MP3s)

Decide what you would like to heal. It can be physical, emotional, mental, or spiritual.

Write it and your bottom line down in your journal.

Call in your power animal. Let it know that you'd like to obtain a healing.

Journey to upper world as you have been taught. When you get there, call out that you have come for a healing.

From that point on, everything that happens will be part of the healing, so try and relax and cooperate as well as remember everything you can.

When you hear the call back beat, journey back the exact way you went and journal the journey and your experience as soon as you are back.

Use your reference books and interpret the journey by translating metaphors and then referring the journey back to your request.

# Chapter X:
# Power Animals and Helping Spirits

**Power Loss**

There is a spiritual illness known as power loss. Normally, power animals and helping spirits come and go in our lives, depending on what we need at the time. Generally we have at least two or three at all times. Sometimes one will leave but another won't come to take its place. This is power loss. Signs that this may have happened include depression, increased incidence of accidents, ill health, as well as indications that things that you need are not manifesting well in your life.

Very often, power loss will accompany soul loss, and the symptoms are very similar. Soul loss is another spiritual illness that was identified and treated by the ancients in which we disconnect from part of our essence or natural expression. It is caused by such things as shock, trauma, and cultural conditioning to name a few.

We all suffer from power loss and soul loss from time to time. If you sneeze or get startled you can have soul loss, although in such cases you generally have spontaneous recovery. Anything more traumatic than that usually results in more prolonged soul loss and requires the help from a trained professional.

The more soul loss and power loss we have, the lower our energy frequency. When our frequency is low, we are less able to manifest in our world, less sure of who and what we are, and we are less able to have healthy boundaries. With extensive power loss and/or soul loss our overall frequency drops so low that eventually we can't even maintain physical health.

**Getting to Know You**

It is really important to spend time with your power animals and helping spirits, being with them in journey space. Frolic and play with them, feed them, pet them, and converse with them often. Also, inviting them to merge (shape shift) with you in ordinary reality helps you get familiar with each other. It also helps you align with the power they represent.

I have often wondered when I see children pretending to be animals or superheroes if this isn't what is going on. I remember "being" a horse as a young girl and really experiencing what it felt like to jump a fence.

Non-ordinary reality is so vast and all encompassing that we can lose ourselves in it. Doing personal journeys to explore it and acquaint yourself with your animals and helpers can help you avoid getting disoriented later when you are doing journeywork for a specific purpose.

While on exploratory journeys, you can ask questions of your animals and spirits while in a relaxed state. It really helps you align with their energies, and it can be really healing for both of you to do this. Giving them gifts and thanking them is also important. They are just waiting out there to help you. When you're lost or confused during a journey, or in ordinary reality for that matter, notice how they are right there waiting for you to ask for their help.

Once I was out in a remote wilderness area on a ten-day, solo-backpacking excursion. I was lying on a hillside, it was a beautiful day, and there was a raven soaring above me. I felt relaxed and was getting somewhat mesmerized by the breeze and the sun on my face, after my morning's hike. The raven was playing in the air currents apparently just for the pure joy of it.

I began to think about what it would be like to ride the wind, to do a wingover and soar. Pretty soon I had a deep longing to know what a raven in flight experiences.

I whimsically addressed the raven and said, "I'd really like to know what it would be like to be you."

I was suddenly looking down at myself. I could feel the wind in my feathers and what it was like to make just the tiniest of a shift in a primary feather and bank. I looked down and could see my human body laying down there on the ground. I could see what was up over the next hill that I had yet to climb.

The next day, when I hiked over that hill, I found exactly what I'd seen from the air when I'd been the raven even though the small open park was not on the topographical maps I had been consulting.

## Shape Shifting

This is a very old and ubiquitous shamanic practice. Master shamans reportedly would literally turn into animals. This is not something I have ever done nor have I witnessed it. Yet, somehow I don't think it would overly surprise me to see it happen.

A more common form of shape shifting is empathizing with an animal or person so strongly that you have their experience. You so align with them that you become one with your awareness. It is if (and may be that) your spirit leaves your body and goes into the body of the other. Your body doesn't change, but the essence of who you are goes and joins them. This is probably most effective when you have an invitation from the individual. If you put out your intention, even longing to be like an animal or with it, the animal may respond and pull you into it.

> **Just Clay**
>
> Matter is truly clay
> And follows spirit
>
> Yet we think of it
> As already fired
> Set in stone
>
> With spirit
> Trapped inside
>
> ~ Gwilda Wiyaka ~

It is important to afford animals the same courtesy that you do people, in that you try not to align with or enter the space of an animal or person without first obtaining their permission. Due to the language barriers, this may seem a bit odd at first but as you become more familiar with journey space, getting and recognizing permission becomes easier and more natural.

### ~ Our belief systems age us and trap us in our bodies ~

You can also align with the energies of animals, using a skin or skull. This is done by centering yourself, dropping into a journey space, and then allowing yourself to become fluid.

This is a "letting go" of your own patterning. Matter is then shifted by your intention to align with the animal. You don't leave your body and become the animal; you imprint the animal into you. You soften your frequency signature and then align with what is present in the skin or skull, knowing that energetically the DNA is present there. You allow your energetic form to form around that of the animal.

When you're done, be mindful to reverse the process giving the energy back and returning to your own design. What you're doing is shapeshifting energetically.

As we heal and become more whole, we can afford to be more fluid without losing ourselves.

This is the same process used by some shamanic practitioners when they are doing healing work for another and empathize with them in order to better understand what is going on with their client. The practitioner so aligns with the client that they experience in their own personal body, emotions, sensations or even the thoughts of their client. I call individuals that are very adept at this, empaths.

Trees and other flora can also be power beings that help us, as can minerals and crystals. The modern practice of assigning birthstones may have come from these roots. We can align with anything in nature and receive help and balance, if we learn to work consciously with it.

# Chapter XI:
# Power Animal and Helping Spirit Assignments

**Power Animal Journey Assignment:**

**Honoring**

30 - minute Journey (www.FindYourPathHome.com/store.html)
(Track 3 on "On Wings of Spirit" or "Betwixt and Between" CDs or MP3s)

In this journey you will spend time with your power animals and learn how to better work together.

Call in your power animal. Let it know that you'd like to learn to better work with it or another power animal of your choice and ask to be taken to lower world to do so.

*You may include a bottom line such as: "Given that I want to become a shamanic practitioner" or "Given that I want to better serve my massage clients" or "Given that I want to live in the shamanic way."*

Journey to lower world as you have been taught. When you get there, call out to your power animal.

When your power animal shows up, ask it:

1. What it would like to be called
2. How it would like to have you call it to you when you are calling in your power
3. How you can better work together
4. What specifically it has come to help you with
5. How it would like to be represented on your altar or otherwise (talisman, charm, picture)

*If you feel you may not be able to remember all you are told or shown, use the "in and out journey method" discussed earlier.*

When you hear the call back beat, thank your power animal. If it is not the one you journey with, say goodbye and journey back the exact way you came with your original power animal. Journal the journey as soon as you return.

Use your reference books and interpret the journey by translating metaphors and then referring the journey back to your request.

Repeat this exercise for each of your power animals.

**Helping Spirit Journey Assignment:**

**Communing**

30 - minute Journey (www.FindYourPathHome.com/store.html)
(Track 3 on "On Wings of Spirit" or "Betwixt and Between" CDs or MP3s)

In this journey you will spend time with your helping spirits and learn how to better work together.

Call in your power animal. Let it know that you'd like to learn to better work with the helping spirit of your choice and ask to be taken to upper world to do so.

*Again, you may include a bottom line such as: "Given that I want to become a shamanic practitioner" or "Given that I want to better serve my massage clients" or "Given that I want to live in the shamanic way."*

Journey to upper world as you have been taught. When you get there, call out to your helping spirit.

When your helping spirit shows up, ask it:

1. What is his or her name
2. How they would like to have you call them to you when you are calling in your power
3. How you can better work together
4. What specifically they have come to help you with
5. How they would like to be represented on your altar or otherwise (talisman, charm, picture)
6. Where they are from

*If you feel you may not be able to remember all you are told or shown, use the "in and out journey method" discussed earlier.*

When you hear the call back beat, thank your helping spirit, say goodbye and journey back the exact way you came. Journal the journey as soon as you return.

Use your reference books and interpret the journey by translating metaphors and then referring the journey back to your questions and bottom line.

Repeat this exercise for each of your helping spirits.

**Follow Up Assignment:**

Practice the things you learned from the power animal and helping spirit journey:

1. Get the things recommended for your altar or pictures, etc. For more information on building your alter see: **Sanctuary: The Shamanic Art of Sacred Space By Gwilda Wiyaka available at** www.FindYourPathHome.com/store.html or at www.Amazon.com
2. Practice calling them into your daily life as instructed.
3. Journey to them and play with them often.


**~ May you be blessed with knowledge and comforted with love ~**

Happy Journeys!

Gwilda Wiyaka

## About Path Home Shamanic Arts School

**Path Home Shamanic Arts School** is a unique Colorado State Certified Occupational School designed to bring into modern times and healing practices the ancient, tried and true shamanism skills of our indigenous peoples. At Path Home, we understand that there is a growing need for well-trained spiritual healers and stewards in our modern communities.

**Path Home** offers an intensive Shamanic Practitioner Certification Program specifically designed to prepare our students to build their private practice treating spiritual illness. Our graduates are trained to enter the professional world interfacing with mainstream health care practitioners. The Shamanic Practitioner Certification training is a two-year, 386-hour program that produces competent, well prepared shamanic practitioners to treat the spiritual illness of today's people.

The **Path Home Shamanic Instructors Certification Program** trains individuals to teach shamanic skills through the use of shamanic techniques. In order to effectively teach the practice you need to not only be proficient in the form itself, but be able to track your students in non-ordinary reality. Path home teaches its instructors this and many other unique skills creating exceptional teachers.

**Map Home** is a branch of Path Home that offers classes, workshops and healing retreats for individuals interested in personal growth and development, and in learning to live in a shamanic way. During these intense, rapidly changing times through 2012 and well beyond, Path Home prides itself in supporting spiritual evolution by preparing individuals to not only survive but to thrive in the newly emerging landscape.

For more information on Path Home Shamanic Arts School, Map Home Personal Growth Programs, or to find a **Path Home Certified Shamanic Practitioner** contact us:

www.FindYourPathHome.com
TouchIn@FindYourPathHome.com
303-775-3431

# About Path Home's State Certification

Path Home Shamanic Arts School is a Colorado State Certified Occupational School. This means that Path Home has gone through a rigorous certification program that insures its founder, director, and instructors have the qualifications to teach the shamanic arts. In addition, the student's interests are guarded with bonded tuition to certified curriculum and established refund policies. The catalogs and all four certification programs are approved and on file with the state of Colorado; this insures consistency and quality of the classes.

Why did we go through all the expense, paper work, scrutiny, and time to obtain certification from the State of Colorado for Path Home?

- In order to teach anything in the State of Colorado that can be used in an existing job or as a job, certification by the state is legally required.

- Integrity: Integrity was and is our core motivation for creating the School. The Shamanic Arts are a viable powerful healing modality that requires extensive training as well as personal growth and development to wield responsibly. Spiritual healing is, in its own way, as complex as physical healing. For this reason, we feel it is irresponsible in the extreme to perform spiritual healings after having learned a few techniques at workshops.

- While the physical and emotional/mental healing arts are regulated as of yet, the spiritual ones are not. For this reason, Path Home has chosen to hold itself to the exacting standards we feel the field not only warrants but deserves.

- Path Home Shamanic Arts School trains and certifies "Shamanic Practitioners" not "Shaman". We feel that the indigenous shaman from all cultures are in a class all their own and we do not profess to offer in two years what takes life times and generations to achieve.

- Our programs are designed to produce competent well trained Shamanic Practitioners of integrity to take on the spiritual illnesses of our culture today. It is for this reason we feel that our program needs to stand up to the quality and exacting standards of today's educational systems.

Path Home's listing with The Division of Private Occupational Schools (DPOS):
www.highered.colorado.gov/DPOS/Students/directory.asp?residency=in

# Resources

## CDs and MP3s available for this workbook

**On Wings of Spirit** (quad drumming for the shamanic journey)
**Betwixt and Between** (double drumming for the shamanic journey)

Available at: www.FindYourPathHome.com/store.html

## Shamanic Healing

Path Home offers long distance shamanic healing sessions.
To schedule an appointment with a Path Home certified shamanic practitioner contact us:

www.FindYourPathHome.com
TouchIn@FindYourPathHome.com
303-775-3431

## Additional books, CDs, and MP3s by Gwilda

Available at: www.FindYourPathHome.com/store.html

## Books:

### Sanctuary, The Shamanic Art of Sacred Space: Workbook 2

The easily understood shamanic principles and techniques found in **Sanctuary** offer step by step instruction on creating sacred space for the home or workplace. This book is a must read for anyone seeking peace and personal empowerment.

## CDs & MP3s:

**On Wings of Spirit** (quad drumming for the shamanic journey)
**Betwixt and Between** (double drumming for the shamanic journey)

**One People One Nation** (ancient and modern shamanic songs)
**Winds of Time** by StarFaihre (ancient and modern shamanic songs)

Notes

Notes

Notes

Notes

Notes

www.ingramcontent.com/pod-product-compliance
Lightning Source LLC
LaVergne TN
LVHW081400060426
835510LV00016B/1914